Starting Preschool

This book belongs to

_____

"Children need to talk about change;
use this book as a tool to connect with your child
and color the pictures together."

Jo Crowley

First published in Brisbane, Australia by Color My Story Pty Ltd August 2011

© Copyright 2011 Color My Story Pty Ltd

Text © 2011 Jo Crowley
Illustrations © 2011 Nadya Constantinidis

Starting Preschool

My name is

_____

I have _____ eyes

I have _____ hair

I like _____

_____

_____

_____

I have some exciting news.

Soon I will start ....

at ....

I will be going _____ days a week.

My days will be:

Monday

Tuesday

Wednesday

Thursday

Friday

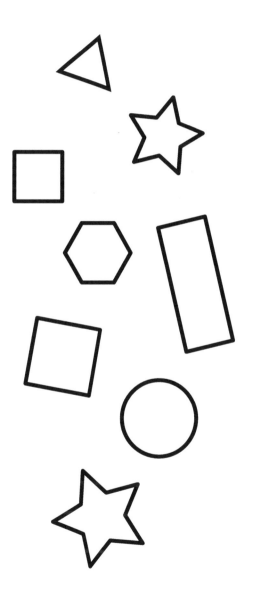

In the morning
I will help get ready.

We will pack

_____

_____

_____

_____

_____

I will brush my hair,
brush my teeth and
put my shoes on.

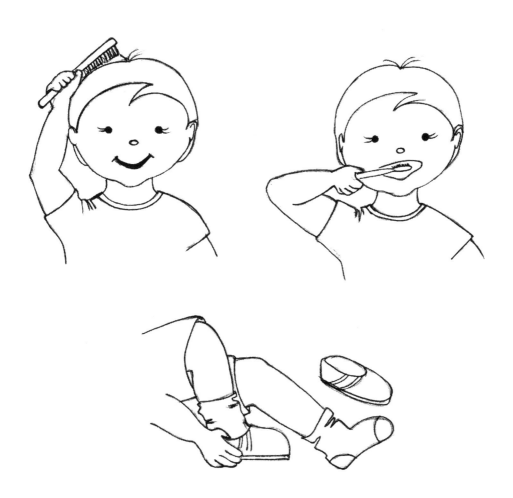

When we arrive we will say hello.

Then we will sign in
and unpack my bag.

When we are inside there will
be lots of things to learn while
I play with my new friends.

Outside there will be
new things to learn
and explore.

There will be an area where I can go
to the bathroom and wash my hands.

We will have yummy food to eat.
I will sit and eat with my friends.

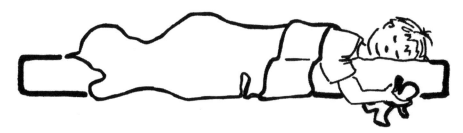

During the day there will be time to rest.
I will lay down on a bed just for me
and close my eyes.

If I feel sad I can talk to my teachers or someone at home.

At the end of the day I will be picked up to go home. I can tell everyone at home about my fun day.

Going to preschool
is very exciting.

Meeting new friends is lots of fun.

My First Day

The friends I played with are

Today I ate

Outside I played

Inside I played

I chose to play with

PHOTOS / DRAWINGS / COLLAGE OF MY FIRST DAY

PHOTOS / DRAWINGS / COLLAGE OF MY FAMILY

Other books in this series

Moving House
Written by Jo Crowley
Illustrated by Jayne Croft

Mommy Has A Baby In Her Tummy
Written by Jo Crowley
Illustrated by Jayne Croft

Starting School
Written by Jo Crowley
Illustrated by Jayne Croft

Pieces Of My Puzzle
Written by Jo Crowley
Illustrated by Nadya Constantinidis

Divorce/Separation

Printed in Great Britain
by Amazon